BLACK EMERALDS

by

Rais Neza Boneza

I am moribund
But in my drunkenness of death
Rests the breast of the moon
That feeds my man's heart

Black Emeralds

Rais Neza Boneza

Cyberwit.net
HIG 45, KAUSHAMBI KUNJ,
KALINDIPURAM,
ALLAHABAD - 211011 (U.P.)
INDIA +(91) 9415091004

E-mail: info@cyberwit.net
www.cyberwit.net

ISBN 10: 81-8253-034-2
ISBN 13: 978-81-8253-034-8
First Edition : 2005
Rs. 200/-

DEDICATION

To my friends…

Aksanti! to Dr. Marisa Antonaya for her dedication in promoting peace through literature. Aksanti ! to Kjell Olaf Jensen of the Norwegian Pen for the sense of justice, you given to us in exile. Aksanti again!

THE AUTHOR

Rais Neza Boneza was born on 29 July 1979 in the Democratic Republic of the Congo. Currently, he lives in exile in Norway. He is an artist, writer, poet and peace activist. Rais Boneza's book is a magnificent tribute to human dignity and solidarity. The author is able to keep a sense of hopefulness while conveying the inner turmoil experienced by a human in exile fleeing the horrors of war. Being in exile, he recalls his memory and dreams of hope, love and passion while the world is still in torment. Most poems present a successful mixture of the universal and the particular, and as a result most readers will be able to identify with the main character as he goes through his search for freedom and wholeness. His writing has been published in different magazines worldwide. His publications include:

    - Nomad a refugee poet, cookcommunication USA 2003

    - Peace by Africans' peaceful means, proteapublishing USA 2004

CONTENTS

NANDI.. 9

I AM THERE, AND THERE I REMAIN 10

THE BANK OF MISERY 12

GLOBAL TORMENT 13

THE PRESENCE 16

FOR WISDOM NOT POSSESSED 17

THE SURVIVOR 18

THE WORSHIPPER 20

EARTHLY TREADMILL OF PAIN 22

MATERIALISTS 23

FRIENDSHIP 24

MY DEAREST PEARL 25

HUMANITY 26

ROUTE TO TRØMSØ 27

ON THE SUMMIT OF DESPAIR 28

UNTITLED 29

SEASONS 30

MY BLOMSTER FLOWER 31

THE BATTLE OF BIRDS 32

MY ISLAND 33

BALLAD OF NIAGARA 34

LE FÉLIN 35

MIDNIGHT 36

THE INKS OF MY FACE 37

FIGHT FOR LAND 39

MESSENGER OF JOY 40

UNTITLED 41

OLD BEAUTY 42

BEYOND BORDERS 43

ABOVE THE SEA 44

UNTITLED 46

BLACK ESMERALDA 47

THE WORLD 48

UNTITLED 49

ORPHEUS'S LAST WORDS 50

WHEN THE TIME ARISES 51

THE GENESIS OF APOCALYPSE 52

THE FLIGHT OF PEGASUS 54

THE LAST FLOWER 55

UNTITLED 56

UNTITLED 57

THE FALL OF MY DREAMS 58

UNTITLED 59

THE RUNNER 60

THE BIRTH OF THE SUN 62

LITTLE BROTHER 63

DOULEUR 64

Nandi

I have reached my destination, and I continue to write. My quill seems to pour its ink **onto** the banks of the Tanganyika Lake. The sacred place to which - from the other side of the border - I confided my boredom and worries when I was younger. But always hence a long my way.

How have I arrived at the *kraal* of the **oldest wisdom,** Bashingatahe ?

These legendary characters armed with virtues, keepers of the tradition of tolerance; as I've been told – this is also a story, or yet another imagining. But I am as often inspired and consoled by the lake; we always went there together. We are from the lake, she and I.

She who freed me every morning from the prison of the subconscious that shrouded me whenever languid sleep appeared on the horizon. She writes too. She writes verses in the sand on the beach, or draws figures in the water on the lake. We are from the lake, she and I .

We are very close because we had the lakes in common, our nuptial bed. We are united, almost intimate, and love had never been so noble. She and I together in the lake that nourishes our desires, passion and freedom.

Nandi belongs to the lake, a beauty that surpassed that of the Muses. And in her eyes, as on the shores of the lake, I found my freedom.

- Nandi has fallen asleep, and I watch **over her-**

I Am There, And There I Remain

The Promises **pass from mouth** to mouth. Like palm wine, tainted, almost **overtaking** the final thirst of the drunkard of political propaganda. A large **dose** of poisonous wine fed to an entire, vulnerable people to deepen their eternal ignorance.

The earth is in misery. All around, hypocrisy guides spirits, and the souls beneath bleed out of hate. The family cell has already been infected. **Clan** nepotism kills my homelands like the Ebola virus. In our regions, **we make enemies for ourselves**. Neighbours, friends, brothers, men and women: we are all enemies to one another. And in the end, we are left alone in the solitude of immorality. But I am there…

Aaaaaaaaaaaah…a sudden growl

Startled, I jump away from the abyss of my confused thoughts. The voice that clearly rages against the tedium of an entire world. Cloistered in the grave of hope, there is nothing more astounding than the grievances of humans in disarray. One is stifled, and one survives. The heat is soporific. In this place the imagination is great, and we dream of snow, that graceful northern dust we can only see **reflected** on the high peak of mount Ruwenzori. It is a place of sublime freedom, where our souls take off in astral flight towards the highest reaches of freedom. Here, we are creators. We are gods and **goddesses** in a paradise that no executioner can take from us. Our Dreams. It is a place of suffering and sorrow. And I am there…

I am a criminal, sentenced **for** being myself, the son of my mother and of my father; what will I be tomorrow? Yet, tomorrow doesn't exist. And today is the **inheritance** of the times that have come before. The world where one revolution follows another in endless succession; a world shaped by fear and terror. And there I remain.

There was a moment when my friend **in** misfortune stared wordlessly at me; by his pale beard it was clear that he had been taken in as a special guest in that home of torments. His dry eyes pierce my pounding heart. He looks at me, a smile appears on his face; and then, a tremendous burst of laughter. A shiver of coldness passing through my body snuggled into the deepest corner our **space**. He suddenly becomes quiet, invoking a chaotic silence. He points a finger and says to me:

You haven't done anything either, eh?

The Bank of Misery

Eighteen days since the Ship began its voyage towards Kinshasa, on the majestic river Zaire (Congo); travelling slowly and hesitantly on this viscous liquid leaving behind the foretold fall of a regime.

We have tamped everything down under the sacks of Cassava, Unimaginable condition under the barges. Solitary; even the torrential equatorial rains that fall on us always choose the time when the shadow of night appears ; while under the torrid sun, the tse-tse flies show us no compassion.

Krak! This is a surprise, and soon again it is normal. Once again a stop, a bank of sand.

Vandring at over eight hundred kilometres from Boyama (Kisangani) ; once again near Lisala. The brave Dinanga, the ship has thrown itself once again into a sandbank. The passengers piled up among the merchandise are mourning, yes! From mourning to mourning, an everyday **existence** on the Dinanga ship, which has become a haunted place.

The great evils have arrived. Every day one or two depart from life, and we don't know how many have been affected: a death from dysentery, a death from cholera, every day.

Three days have passed, stuck helplessly to the sand, without fuel, in the middle of the river. During this time, things break down in front of us, and behind us.

The state simmers and finally dissolves. We are but a sample of what people from all corners of the country are living. Misery and abandonment. But now, among the bags of manioc, under a trap of wealth, a new victim dies; a friend, a brother who yesterday was well and today finds himself perishing.

His face remains forever etched into my spirit: a man who fights to survive. Alone, a refugee on this boat, attacked by diseases…. his heart wants to let go…

Global Torment

Nowadays at the ascension of this new era, the world seems to have fallen into the prelude of the chaos and plunges towards global barbarism. After the collapse of communism and the cold war, we are now chanting the rhythms of war against terror. Many groups of people in our cynical and blinded world passively have accepted the plans of war and total extermination of women and child of the "third world. Those who believe to have been anointed by God and gods to take life, violate humans and natural laws deliberately.

It is shameful that the "powers-assemblies" continue to prove their unwillingness to resolve conflict and implement peace. Human rights are still unlegislated in large parts of our world. We know where the devil is coming from. Poor and miserable people are ignored and marginalized by corporate media who collaborate in the selfish foreign policy of "western" and "owned-governments" who savagely victimize the poor in the majority world through their form of globalization. Globalization is a worldwide nest of injustice and terror. More than a billion inhabitants of the earth live under the threshold of misery and desolation.

We can clearly see that the enraged thirst for war under the guise of the war against terrorism or the fight against evil does not make world healthy at all and. Instead of using their power and resources for peace and justice in the world, the "wealthiest of clan of men and women" above humanity tend to legitimize the practice of terrorism by waging meaningless wars, suffocating people economically; one wonders who is a terrorist and who is not. We assist the globalization of barbarism which leads to greater economic concentration and financial power in the hands of the minority while the number of excluded and poor grows dramatically. Globalization has changed the agenda of all national and internal institutions. The world economy is based on maximizing profit. We are faced with an economic system that has an imperative of money and profit by any means and where human values have no place. We should remember that when society does not consider the human needs, the lack of a future creates feelings of insecurity, individualism, and greed. Violence increases, giving rise to movements based on anger and hatred. Millions of women, men and children have lost their life since the all the time and until today, the culmination of centuries of violence.

The only instrument which has been easily globalized is the gun, symbolized by the "Kalashnikov" and the green paper used to buy it. Even in remote parts of the world in deep forest rural people use guns for deadly purposes. The propaganda of unscrupulous leaders with an uncontrolled thirst for financial gain and the control of oil under the cover of neutralization of weapons of mass destruction justify war and massacres of innocent civilians. Those leaders are the first to sustain and finance the trade of weapons with countries who once were allies and later were branded enemies.

History reveals that there were no weapons of mass destruction in the Balkans, Afghanistan or in Iraq, only more than a hundred thousand innocent victims. The past century in Rwanda more than a million lost their life; in the Republic Democratic of Congo more than four million people died and the genocide continues in the central Africa region and around the globe. And there are forgotten elsewhere, the plight of people in the Nagaland, Darfur, Somalia, or the Ivory Coast.

The many, who lost their lives before and after the twins tower in New York - were they victims of these so-called weapons of mass destruction? We should remember that the new empire were first used nuclear weapons and today depleted uranium weapons, a form of nuclear warfare, were used and are being used in Yugoslavia, Afghanistan and Iraq and leave a lasting effect on local populations and their environment. Let us not be distracted by the lies of those unlawful governments. What a shame for lands that has produced such leaders as Dr. King or Gandhi and are still waging meaningless violence and oppressing the weak. Well, they did not understand the lesson.

We have told that democracy is based on truth, clarity and liberty. The people of the world have to unite in solidarity and help each other to create a culture of peace as universal based on equality and human dignity. There is a need for international and national institutions to resolve conflict. We need to remove eminent threat of nuclear war and extinction. Since war and many other problems are global, we need a global agency like U.N. with integrity and legitimacy to enforce laws and to maintain peace. We need first to globalise justice.

We need to go beyond national boundaries to a world agency with legal and moral accountability and credibility. We need a new understanding of nature; only if we respect and preserve nature will we preserve ourselves. Instead of respecting and implementing resolutions adopted by the United Nation, our leaders lie and fabricate any excuse for waging war. Now is the time for us, as belonging to the environment and citizens of the world to take responsibility for the destiny of our humanity if we want peace and sustainability for future generation.

Remember that as long as misery and poverty exist, the world will never experience any time of rest or security. Even if we try to construct walls or shields against, we shall never be in peace. Food and dignity for all are prerequisites for global justice and equality.

THE PRESENCE

And I felt in the bottomless air
A wind that disturbs my being
With a joy of sublime thoughts
A sense of elevated nature
Of something far more deeply mixed
In my impression, I duel
In the light of the setting sun
Around the ocean and the bowing breath of life
So bluest of deepest firmament of my world,
And I say: I have seen a light

FOR WISDOM NOT POSSESSED

To understand the whims
Secrets and thoughts of mortals
Then to control his hand
Soul and mind
To clean this man thoughts of hatred
And get him out of the stupid quarrels
Of human nature
Make him not a disciple of war
Before he makes that choice too late

THE SURVIVOR

War is treasure of all tendencies
Why if I could be just a mere vegetal
Or a rock in the middle
Of dry sand and steppes

War-
War-
And war-

I see you everywhere
And nowhere

My dream,
You interfere
My visions are blinded
My quietness not better
My gifted-privileges so bitter
And disregarded,
I am—

Today, they say to me:
We give you democracy
Alas! They have given me
Their freedom
Bureaucracy!
The civilization's boredom

They do not see the pain
Neglected from a land of his own

Heir of sorrow
Freed in a world of human's machinery
I play the "far-south"

And at the end my mother
Do not understand yet—
I survive my wars
To die from peace

THE WORSHIPPER

I climb the hill of my feelings
To satisfy my sight.
I seek to find, my reason is lost.
In my estrangement my soul speaks.

Abandoned as a discarded plant
I look to thee;
All thy greatness is in my sight.
You leave your dwelling
As thy sun seeks its resting place.

I am rooted to your very being;
My branches cover your presence;
You move under my shadow.

I understand with the vigor of thought,
Thy body but with a glance.
I admire you without weariness
And explore you from discovery to wonder.

I praise thy sculptor,
Him, the all-wise, the all-bestower
Who, beneath the pounding of my misled heart,
Long ago fashioned your existence
For the accomplishment of compassion
And the gift of the essence of love.

I am the spirit who observes you;
You do not know me,

Yet you are a reality well known by me.

Source of poetic water from above,
Inspirational rain from the sky,
From thee my feelings are nurtured
Even in thy obscurity of me.

My words remain silent,
And for thee my existence still a fable,
A dream that I shall never share,
A poem never to be written.

EARTHLY TREADMILL OF PAIN

Why was she born?
To lead an empty life
Why was she born?
In this world of rock and sand
Yet she craves places, which others also crave
Because she did love her beloved one
Do you think she doesn't suffer?
It's hopeful that you have seen the taboo:
Her love the only source of his strength
Why was I born? she asks.
Sweating blood and water from her soul
Maybe she will enjoy the here-after-life
The sweetness of her sin of love —

MATERIALISTS

Men and women with neither wisdom
Nor humour full of pride and arrogance
They are like a ship sailing to its doom
Their S.O.S emergency calls
Are never answered—

FRIENDSHIP

Look in my eyes
Grab my soul and heart
Compassion within belongs to you
I hear your deepest silence
Listen to the melody of my desire for you:

Through the voyage of life
We travel along courses and smooth paths
Some bumpy with pot notes
But do not you ever despair
A sparking light gleams the darkest gloom

MY DEAREST PEARL

Cry you not—Weary you not
For loneliness, turbulences, doubts and failure
Are just mere illusion
Reality is the special bond we share
Laughter, happiness, fulfillment
Are only inches of my outstretched arm
You fall, I catch you
You are lost, you find me
Friend now friend ever

HUMANITY

Political isms for sale
For anybody to make a tale
Humanism is but a name
An echo in a crowded silence for fame
Is humanity to see
Children wedded with misery
Sick and drunk of poverty
Refugees in their own land?
Is it to make air-raids
Bomb innocent people
And wage war against nature
To blackmail its creature?
Merchants of humanity
In black gowns
Pity roses from the world
And you preach starvation
For the destroyed nation

ROUTE TO TRØMSØ

The Odin's wind blows
Chasing the sun through the clouds in panic
Until they cover the sky with a cold shadow
Between the *trærne* trees
The little *elva* river flows and birds sing a solstice melody

And between the freezing vegetation
Breezes hail at me:
Put on a warm robe
How can you expose yourself
To the kissing breath of the weather?
Enter your dwelling
Rest by her warm side
And plunge in the boiling pleasure of your twins-passion.

That why the route- to-the north is cold
Because the sun shines there too
For men and women to burn in love—

ON THE SUMMIT OF DESPAIR

I am a very salted tear
When you drink me
You will never be thirsty

I flow endlessly
I am a brutal fall
In a bottomless space

When you drink me twice
You are drunk for two centuries
When you drink me three times
You are drunk for three centuries

And four times…
Then you are an eternal drunkard

UNTITLED

After thousand nights under Bombs
The children reached the heaven today morning
They are among the million who sing
In the golden hair of the Sun

SEASONS

The paths make love
Tenderly and passionately
The stars make love too
In the only bed of Gods mixed with Gods
Who make love—

The trees go around kissing each other
In their natural madness

In their wild excitement
Winds blow in a nuptial flight

The Soul of the moon in the soul of the lake
The soul of the sun in the soul of the child
I reject the universal dance for that woman
I throw away the deadly stones—

MY BLOMSTER FLOWER

I am born from your eyes

Lovely sun

I wear that silhouette

I dwell in your fertile heart

Fruitful with thousands stars

Between thousand eternal happiness

Slowly-

Softly-

I flounder between your hidden lips

Coloured with rainbow colours

I die to rise up with tears of joy

I die to live

THE BATTLE OF BIRDS

Bird of fire, Bird of love
If only I could know…
Free to fly by your Side in the Azure without measure of despair
I did not see to rival the bird of evil
In the struggle, you sunk
And by his cruel beak, he stabbed my soul

Bird of fire, bird of love
In the abyss without bottom of despair
I am succumbed by you, death
As neither heaven, nor times known
To relieve my pain
With the strength of legends, now I call:

Bird of fire, bird of light
While for you the love burns in my soul
I shall wait whatever the torments
Because affection is inscribed in my heart
My ashes mixed with my tears
Now are reborn like phoenix.

MY ISLAND

O my island
Your eyes are two suns
Who cover me and enlighten me
Your breasts are two hills of crystal
They attract me
 From the deepest of your soul
Ever virgin your body and heart
Run a refreshing source, pure honey
And with my all-being
Flies my eternal breath:
    I love you

BALLAD OF NIAGARA

If I am

A breeze blowing above the impalpable air

If I am

A song

Then neither barrier, nor frontier

My style is born from humanity

Coming from profundity of inspirations

I hunt the corners and emotions of this world

If I am

Singing birds

I brew the spirit and I pierce every side

Song and Ballad mix with the free melodic verbs

And waves of instrument crossing the soul

Imposing cheerfulness

Shield against enmity

If then,

I am what a melody is all about

As the fall of Niagara

The flow of the poet purifying humankind

LE FÉLIN

I tasted the bitter happiness of your lips
I tasted the illusory happiness of your heart
In your folly, I learned to be a man
I learned to knock with strength
Where I was soon caressing

MIDNIGHT

My bedroom
Feeling
Smocks
Smell
Anxiety

It midnight past two
At midnight two minutes

THE INKS OF MY FACE

O! Pharaoh of torment.
I would like to show you
How much you have betrayed the son of kundalini
How much you abuse our mother earth

Alas! My words are dumbfounded
I don't have the easy verb of the Mahatma,
He had the word to move mountains.

As Caesar advances through Jerusalem
To enslave sons and daughters of Eve
Unfortunately, we lack the bravery of Jeanne D'arc
From her womb,
The dignity of a nation was born

Why my world has lost its wisdom?
It surely misses the knowledge of Daimoshin
Or the vibrating verb
And the teaching of Baha'u'llah
To realize unity, peace and prosperity
For those million of children who never laugh.

Alas! I am still in exile,
In *Odin's* land
Where I listen the *Kora* of the Sami
To forget the raising thousand tears
Of the Nile River setting sun

Well! The source of my *larmes dries up*

While, I hear the new unborn wailing

Thus divinities from the Pleiades
Borrow me the inks of their eyes
To change the flowing destiny of our history

FIGHT FOR LAND

The fight for wisdom
Ends up in darkness
Like our past fellow revolutionaries
Now where is our land?
Borders-Frontiers-Barriers
Blinding our spirits with selfishness....

MESSENGER OF JOY

As a thief in the night
Nobody can predict his assault
As a storm coming from near-far
Nobody can hinder his approach.
Why the Grief?
In the coldness of Darkness
Light in its splendour blankets us
With the warmth of our lowly condition.
The harbinger of the end
Is but the herald of a rebirth

UNTITLED

Akeba has found her way to the lake
Where lies the last breeze of Maketa.
She too is a daughter of Llyr

OLD BEAUTY

A flight of times,
A flight of petals,
The wind blows,
The perfect fades
Charms vanish.
Endless smartness,
Eternal sensuality,
O wild beauty!
The world adores your youthfulness,
We celebrate the death of time.

BEYOND BORDERS

The souls wait for the angels
Those who take away
The breath of the sentenced nations
The men of the Empire—-
The Soul-taker

Beyond our borders
Horizons decay
Nations perish in the abysses of silence

Beyond our borders
Behind us
The last empire decays surely.

ABOVE THE SEA

I sit on the edge of the sea without name
I observe...
In search for a forgotten memory

Yet!
I am born again
When I look at the sea
A sea without name
And you set me free

I leave my reflection in your ocean
To escape the pain of my pleasure
And you fall in the drowned water of my hands

In the breath of the nameless sea
My memory is buried
And forgotten.

No—
Never forgotten—

A sermon of eternity lies in
For the souvenir
Of those moments that shaped my soul

And now above the Sea
My happiness will sail
Upon the Undulant breezes

And always the *ship* of remembrances
Will sail upon waves of happiness
During night of times

UNTITLED

Where is the source of peace?
Where is the light of compassion?

Hopefully not far from our hearts
In the temple of our sons and daughters
Lies the altar of Sharing and Justice
The Bread and wine of reconciliation
Ready for our relief for eternities.

BLACK ESMERALDA

Following the light of the sky,
the star remains so far in the spaces,
alone in the garden of flickering lamps;
we talk to thee, my spark.

Thee, black, yet a golden rose;
Emerald of delighted lands,
desiring to kiss your sombre skin,
but the thorns around thee prevent me.

In your indifference,
You reach for setting sun.
You wait for Orpheus, the enchanter.

We didn't see the approach
Of the current of circumstances
Flowing with you towards the falls of uncertainty.

Oh! White dove, seen yet untouchable.
Our eyes still fixed on one sacred desire;
With thee we want to share our treasure of love,
But our kingdoms are waging war.

We are the deprived princes in exile
On our mount, Pegasus,
Riding from galaxy to galaxy.

For you, Esmeralda,
I am a breath that silently passes by.
My rose, my fragrant flower,
I am but for you:

"A memory that has been born dead."

THE WORLD

Does it flow from source to cataracts?
Is it like a light in a crowded darkness?
Is it a tragedy?
Or a mixture of hell and paradise?
A mirror reflecting the chaos
Or an hourglass behind immemorial bars?

What, Then, it is?

UNTITLED

Rainbow

How can I forget you?

ORPHEUS'S LAST WORDS

Bitterness of life
Be spited off from wombs
And find oneself slave of earthly principles
And succumbing from machinations

Break the chains of bronze
Break the umbilical cordon
Be far from the circle of incest

Alas! The throne judges me guilty
From my ascension
I master the tormented waves
In my guiltiness
Under the providential wing,
Humbly I call:

Men of Athens!

Judge not, that ye be not judged
One single judge, One way, One truth
Your spear of grudge will never reach me
For I am a holy spirit in a holy body.

WHEN THE TIME ARISES

A breath from the fog
A breath from the frightening shadows
A scream terror from their feelings
The tower of Absalom flounders

In the borders of sombre Abysses
In the black chamber
In the dark tunnel
The route to crucifixion

A signature from the bestowed—
The announced end —
Of Babylon

Witness of extinctions
 Suppressed nations

In the shadowed hall
Patiently and fearlessly
In the chaos of their custody
Souls wait Moment to moments
The inevitable approach of the times;
The revenge—
The thirst of the purple fluid —

THE GENESIS OF APOCALYPSE

Sons of Eden
Humans-fruit-sin
Hum! Genius machination

Sons of Abraham
Ishmael
Isaac
Sons of sons
David—
King—
And kings

Bible-Koran-Torah
Words—
Holy words
Hatred—

Genocide,
Massacres
killings

Religion-gods-goddess-God-prophets-sons

Colonization
Apartheid
Racism

In their names
Crusades—Jihad

War-Ta Ta Ta Boom!-Terror

Hum!

And yet heaven and hell still exist

Both in war and desolation

And blood, the foundation of human civilization

"Watch out for angels in the sky!"—Something may happen

THE FLIGHT OF PEGASUS

Deploying his agile wings in the blowing wind
Taking flight in the endless stared darkness
Sailing in the ocean of quietness
In bottomless azure, he glides

Flying horse,
Happy creature,
Exploring secret places
His presence shines in heavy night
The light of his spirit increases
Seeing Prometheus there in distances
From the sight of his admirer
Pegasus, the proud escapes far away

In the deepness of his majestic flight
He edifies the everlasting of his existence
Since released by Alpha
Now swimming in the grace of Gamma
He follows his legend through Omega

THE LAST FLOWER

I gather a flower from your favourite woods
And I embrace it close to my heart
Where you liked to pose on your cheek

I gather this morning the last flower—
The symbol of delicates
And I compare his thin stems
To the delicacy of your fairy fingers.

I gathered this morning a flower —
The aroma is pure of freshness
And I am surprised by dreams
The breath of your perfume

I gathered this morning a flower—
While your absence fills my empty soul
An angel flies by my beside
And I sing the song of my pain

UNTITLED

Babel—
Mother tongue
Humans tower
The source—
Gomorrah tearing

UNTITLED

Thou shall not
Yes! I will
Thou shall not
Yes! I will
Shall you?
No! Will I?

THE FALL OF MY DREAMS

And thus time stands still
My heart no longer dances
Dreams art the steps
I now dance to

With no pity
Time marches on
And destiny evades me
Taking with joy and sorrow

Each escaping grain in an hourglass
Glass brings me closer to the yawning mouth
Of an open grave
Always ready to reduce to ashes
Those who feel the destruction
Of the cruelty of times

O! That the heaven would suspend the seasons
That ceaselessly patrol
The borders of my dream!

Alas! My heart is inflated with Grief
I dream –
I think
Nothing new; same days with one Sun
Same night with joyful stars
My only heart observes the chaos

UNTITLED

Love is in love
Embracing the flame in his arms
And behind death mourns his death-

THE RUNNER

Oh! You my Reason for astonishment
So far and so near at once
Oh! Essence of love, Incense of tropics
Feeling never experienced before

Our paths so parallel
But at the end, so divergent
Evil of our separate ways

Memory reflects your presence
My mysterious, strange acquaintance
Let my soul enjoy the freshness of thought
Let my vision enjoy the gracefulness of walk

Oh! You, Gazelle, so rapid in reflex;
Swiftly my eyes follow
Alas! My powerless sight can't retain you
Since as a spectre, your image always fades
And mind and hearth are empty of you.

Oh! You, my inspiration wine
Allow me to forget you
To run far from you
Since for us
Nobody can control the flow of destiny

Oh! My Ostrich feather
For you, I think only of rapture

Oh! My-longed-for orchid
In the drunkenness of my passion
In the Truth of my distant vision
I affirm with unqualified certitude:
Verily, Thou art the perfect woman.

THE BIRTH OF THE SUN

My tears are the lines of my novel
The characters are rigid
Stiff and ready to act in my cynical scenario
I am the milestone of all misfortunes
Miseries that hunt the running-gods in the firmament
My splendour reaches the stars in the immeasurable spaces
And always declines as I attain *"Isis"* giving birth to *Apollo*

LITTLE BROTHER

Little brother
You are a "man" today
Indoctrinated in their cult of Death
Your nation has sold you to the butcher.

Little Brother
Your confusion is not questioned
But still you ask:
Why am I not at school like other children?
Why is this fear built among nations?
Why am I carrying the swords?
Did Baobab branches and doves have no role to play?

Only one response inscribed in your brain:

"Left and right, Left and right"

Well, you do not need to be a clever boy
To execute orders, Big father told you

"Left and right, left and right"

And silently little brother you reply:

- Please, I wanna go home

DOULEUR

Our fear rises from the uncertainty of Horizons
    It flows in our blood and mind

We have lost faith in the light
    We have lost sense of time
Give us
O! Great comet,
A new life
Behind the Gas chamber